Eve's Red Dress

Eve's Red Dress

poems by

Diane Lockward

To Elizabeth
Glad you were here
tonight – & glad we'll meet
again at the Frost Place.
Diane 6/9/03

Wind Publications
2003

First Edition

International Standard Book Number   1-893239-18-7

Library of Congress Control Number   2002117009

Cover Art: Brian Rumbolo, www.brianrumbolo.com

Acknowledgments

Grateful acknowledgment is made to the following journals in which some of these poems first appeared:

Asphodel: "The Mystery of the Missing Girl"
The Beloit Poetry Journal: "My Husband Discovers Poetry," "Vegetable Love"
Cider Press Review: "Eve Argues Against Perfection"
The Comstock Review: "The Fruitful Woman," "Point Pleasant Beach, 1948"
Confluence: "Waiting for the Streetcar"
Cumberland Poetry Review: "Last Dance"
Edison Literary Review: "Superman Flies," "When News Comes of a Child's Death"
Flyway: "The Missing Remote"
Folio: "Feeding Habits"
Free Lunch: "Crazy Larry"
Journal of New Jersey Poets: "The Blues Going and Coming"
Iris: "She Provides Her Therapist with a History"
The Literary Review: "First Cold"
Louisiana Literature: "After the Stillbirth"
The Louisville Review: "My Father's Garden"
Miller's Pond: "On the Use of Concrete Language," "Reading the Signs"
New Delta Review: "The Changing Room"
North American Review: "Eating My Words"
Paterson Literary Review: "The Barren Woman's Dream"
Poet Lore: "Eve's Diner and Road Stop," "Miscarriage"
Poetry International: "The Letters"
Rattapallax: "Losing the Blues"
Rattle: "The Mathematics of Your Leaving," "The Study of Nature"
Seattle Review: "Cracked"
South Dakota Review: "Her Daughter's Feet"

Spoon River Poetry Review: "Eve's Red Dress"
Two Rivers Review: "The Missing Wife"
U.S. 1 Worksheets: "The Barren Woman's Gift"
Willow Review: "Eve's Own Garden," "Going for the Mail After
    the Storm"
Wind: "The Properties of Light," "Saying It Right"

"Felis Rufus" appeared in the anthology, *Mischief, Caprice, and
Other Poetic Strategies* (Red Hen Press, 2003).

"The Fruitful Woman" was reprinted in the 2002 Her Mark
Calendar (Woman Made Gallery).

"The Letters" was reprinted in *Runes.*

"My Husband Discovers Poetry" was featured on *Poetry Daily*
(www.poems.com) on September 18, 1998, and on *The Writer's
Almanac* (NPR) on March 2, 1999. It was reprinted in *Journal of
New Jersey Poets.*

"Vegetable Love" was featured on *Poetry Daily* on August 14,
1997.

I want to thank my early teachers—Madeline Tiger, Priscilla Orr,
and Renée Ashley—for their wisdom and encouragement. I also
want to express my appreciation to Baron Wormser and Kim
Addonizio who read earlier versions of this manuscript. Much
gratitude goes to all the people at The Frost Place in Franconia,
New Hampshire, poetry haven in the mountains. And thanks to my
children, Wes, Coley, and Lacey, who haven't minded too much
having a mother who asks too many questions. And lastly, I want
to thank my husband, Lew, for his careful attention to the little
things.

For my mother
Barbara Gaines Summerville
1917-1992

Contents

III

IV

V

The rusted gates of Eden still remain,
And archeologists at awful cost
Search for a snakeskin or an apple stain . . .

—Linda Pastan, *The Imperfect Paradise*

I

Eve Argues Against Perfection

And the woman said, The serpent
beguiled me, and I did eat.
                    —Genesis 3:13

Beguiled, my ass. I said no such thing.
You say I lost the gift of Paradise.
I couldn't lose what I never had.

You say the serpent tempted me to eat.
You omit that he entered the Garden
on two legs and walked like a man.

And here's what your story always ignores:
I had pure gold, rare perfume, precious stones,
but Adam hadn't touched me all those years.

Perfection in the Garden didn't mean *that* way.
Not having it and not wanting it
was God's idea of perfection, not mine.

So when that serpent strolled up to the tree,
all upright and fine, he threw off the balance,
and I began to pray, *Oh let him be mine.*

When he held out the apple, so round and lush,
when he stroked it to a keen red glow,
I didn't fall to temptation—I rose to it.

I ate that apple because I was hungry.
I wanted what lay outside Paradise,
a world without the burden of perfection.

Now you call all sinful women my sisters.
I say, let them claim their own damn sins.
The apple may not be perfect, but it's mine.

The Fruitful Woman

Today I dress for you
in scarlet. I am
a tomato, plump
and luscious. I pulsate
with seeds.

Today I clothe myself
in yellow. I am
a peach, succulent
and ripe.

For you, I swathe myself
in gold—all melons, oranges,
tangerines, nectarines.

I am a garden of earthly delights.

I am the apple
you would fall for
a thousand times.

I am the apricot you would die for.

I am all strawberries,
blueberries, raspberries,
and cherries, all these and more.

Today I am royal for you.
I dress in a gown
of purple plum.
Come, lift me out of my skin.

Why I Won't Talk About Orgasms

Because the whole world throbs.
Consider the garden hose.
Let water flow without opening the nozzle,
the hose will thrash and explode in a geyser.
The snake that feeds on animals.
Watch the knot of a gopher
slide through its body, how it undulates.
Quite a flopping about, then *swoosh!*
the gopher's gone. Once I said I was a tomato
pulsating with seeds. You said
that was a lie, tomatoes don't pulsate,
but I say they do. And of course, the muscle
of the heart contracts and expands, sometimes
swells to bursting as when my father's gentle heart
turned violent and attacked him.
The twitch in my eye, tic
in my cheek, ache in my tooth.
Even my refrigerator, its compressor broken
after all these years, shudders and convulses
through the long, hard night.
Blue things throb.
My old boyfriend once said I gave him blue balls,
and they were beating like mad. I thought,
What a beautiful thing to say—*blue balls.*
It made my heart shiver.
In the bluegrass of Kentucky,
in eighteen hundred and eighty-six,

Reverend Fairhurst extolled the trembling things
of this earth, preaching his foot-stomping sermon,
"The Organ in Worship."
Romance novels, light shows, childbirth, a stubbed toe.
The pulsometer pump, its pistonless valves
raising water by steam and pressure alone.
Volcanoes, twisters, earthquakes.
And this migraine, pounding for days,
radiating its aura of light. The orgasm does not
stand alone. It is not a star. It is part of the universe
in which everything pulses and throbs and sometimes
even shakes, rattles, and rolls.

Vegetable Love

My vegetable love should grow
Vaster than empires, and more slow....
      —"To His Coy Mistress," Andrew Marvell

She bought the eggplant because her lover
had said he was leaving, and she'd read
somewhere it was an aphrodisiac,
and she was willing to try anything,
even magic, even vegetables.

She could have bought the eggplant at the grocery store,
but because this was work that mattered,
she drove out into the country
and stopped at a roadside farm stand.
She chose the eggplant with care, the way
she might have picked out a baby or a puppy.
She found the perfect one, long, globular,
and so purple it was almost black.

On the way home, she planned how she might prepare it—
in a cold ratatouille, cubed and sauteed,
split and charcoaled over the grill,
or sliced and marinated in lime juice—
and if it worked, and she knew it would, she'd buy more.

But already it was too late. He was gone.

She remembered how it had been back
at the beginning, when he used to come home
with an armload of greens for salads,
how they would rip, shred, grate, then toss,
and feed each other, and how she had loved him.

She kept the eggplant in the refrigerator,
because although he'd said she'd grown strange,
she hoped he'd miss her and return.

It began to soften, then turned to mush.
It liquefied and leaked all over the shelves.
It grew mold and began to stink.
Each night when he did not come back,
she looked at the sodden mess, noted the changes,
told herself it was just beginning to work.

Why I'm a Vegetarian

I hated my mother's food.
Her minced meat, salisbury steak,
her shepherd's pie tasted like Elmer's Glue
and made me remember cows
led to slaughter.
Worst of all, Sunday's cottage ham,
a chunk of meat hacked off a mud-slick pig
and boiled till flesh fell from the bone.

Father poured the wine and blessed the food
we were about to receive, then the chewing began,
my parents not speaking again,
Father telling me jokes, Mother not laughing
as she passed the Spam, mysterious brick
pried from a can. When I complained, she said,
There's a war going on, as if that
justified Spam.

Her specialty, creamed chipped beef on toast points,
Father called *shit on a shingle,* making Mother cry.
I could have made her happy if I'd eaten her liver,
a slab of purple sautéed iron gray, guaranteed
to make me grow up healthy.

Once for my birthday, she prepared a tongue,
yanked from the mouth of a cow and served
on a platter. *A delicacy,* she said.

Its surface looked rough like sandpaper, its color pink
as my own. A gully ran down the center, tubes
poked out one end. I imagined veins, glossy and blue,
beneath the mound of flesh. Father sliced
our wordless meal, mooing
and mooing till Mother fled the room.

She came back, chin quivering, holding a heart-
shaped cake, its cracks covered with pink frosting,
my name a silver thread of tiny sugar pellets.

The Letters

My father has found the letter,
anonymous and full of obscenities.
Everyday he parks outside school and waits.

Now the boy has written a second letter.
My father drives and yells.

I'm not to open *any* mail from now on.
I'm not to talk to boys.
I'm to stop pouting this instant.
Who do I think I am, Marilyn Monroe?

At the stoplight, I see a woman standing
under a street lamp, her skirt hiked, hair loose
and draped over one eye, lips red and full.

The boy and what he would like to do to me,
the loops and swirls of his *t*'s, *l*'s, and *o*'s—

When my father pulls up to the Asian Delight,
a geisha appears in a purple kimono, her lips
lacquered scarlet, the black bun of her hair
a giant mushroom skewered with a stick.

He goes in for take-out. I wait in the car, patient
concubine of an emperor. He has dressed me
in silk the color of plums.

We will eat with chopsticks
and drink rice wine. He will unravel
my cummerbund and touch
my delicate feet.

Steam rises, the windows mist, the air fills
with the smell of dumplings, lo mein, and wonton
soup. I balance the hot bag on my lap,
the third letter already burning my hip.

I'm Lonely As the Letter X

Poor, neglected X, only two and a half pages
in a dictionary nearly three thousand long.
My lover's gone. I know how it feels
to receive scant attention, to have gifts
ignored. X deserves more.

X is special, a symbol, shouting, *Don't do it!*
And kindly too, warning of dangerous crossings,
strange, dark roads travelled alone.
Mysterious, an unknown quantity—who really knows
what X represents? I wish I were prolific as X,
which goes forth and multiplies: 2x, 5x, 7x.

A kiss. Something over the heart, meaning,
I promise, meaning he can't take it back.
Sex chromosome, X gets what it wants.
And X obliterates, gets rid of what once was.
It marks the spot where something is missing.
I'm thinking about Christmas, how X stands in for Christ,
but isn't Him.

And the music X makes, the joy of X
in my mouth: xylotomous, xanthidium, xanthocephalus.
I accumulate X-es, pile them up,
beguiled by xanthomelanous, xanthophyll, xenopeltide.
X is a changeling, a trickster. It keeps itself crossed,
the way a boy twists his fingers, meaning,

I was only fooling, meaning he takes it back.
I've learned from X, become a shape-shifter myself,
a woman who stands on two straight legs
and now keeps them crossed.

Felis Rufus

When his teacher forces similes,
      my small son writes, *I am wild*
            as a bobcat. He has the sleek

            body, muscular limbs of a cat,
      the salty kiss. Curled in a corner,
he pretends he's a kitten born

blind. Nights, he sleeps like a boy,
      thumb in his mouth, limbs twitching.
            Days, he romps in woods, chases

            chipmunks and birds, comes home
      dusted with duff. He grows greedy
for meat, feeds on chickens, rabbits,

and squirrels, collects feathers
      and bones. His rust-colored hair thickens,
            each day more beautiful, more terrifying.

            Long-legged, feet padded, he ravages
      furniture, prowls the neighborhood
from dawn until dusk. Once he brings

home a lamb, once a young pig. My child
      disappears into the rocky hillside, paces
            the jagged ledge of his difference. Do I

only imagine tufted ears, cheek
ruffs? My lynx-eyed son, my wild
boy. Nothing can hold him.

Sometimes he comes back
as a boy, still calling me *Muvver.*
Sometimes the house fills with the must

of his fur. Sometimes night breaks
with mournful howls, cantillations
come down from cold, dark hills.

Going for the Mail After the Storm

So cold and still no letter from my son.
I turn away from the empty box, notice
one belgian block missing from the driveway,
wrenched like a tooth by the snowplow.

I follow the plow's path across the broken snow,
and there pushed up against my neighbor's curb
find my missing stone. I can't lift it with one hand
and even with two can only carry it back
before I have to let it go.

All day I think about the hole left behind, my son
who doesn't write—the necessity for repair,
the city he's fled to. I feel the weight of granite.

Again I see my son board the plane
for California, see him framed in the doorway,
turned to face us one last time, his eyes frozen
in the tower light's glare. The ground trembles
as the plane lifts him, a wrench of air and wing.

I know my husband will say he can fix this
by himself, will want to merely drop the block
back into its hole, and I'll say it won't stay
unless we cement it down.

Saying It Right

Frankie LaMura, who sat
next to me in biology class,
stood in my living room.
Tough boy off his turf,
he wanted to take me
bowling.
He looked from me
to my mother
to my grandmother
and wanting
the right words
opened his mouth
and said, "Youse goils
is all beautiful."
Frankie who bowled
strike after strike,
his muscular arms
an aphrodisiac,
whose hands trembled
when we sliced open
our frogs and when
he touched me—
Frankie LaMura who
in the backseat
of a souped up '59 Chevy
asked me to
correct his grammar,

as if I could fix a boy
the way I might
fix a sentence—
Frankie who had eyes
black as olives,
who wore pressed slacks
for me, who I wanted
in jeans, to whom
I wanted to say only,
Shut up and kiss me,
who kept kissing
long after I stopped
keeping score—
Frankie whose broken
English fixed everything
wrong when I
was seventeen,
whose eyes, lips,
and hands said all
I wanted to hear.

The Flavor of Sadness

[Alex] conducted [Tess] to the fruit-garden and
green-houses where he asked if she liked strawberries.
"Yes," said Tess, "when they come."
        —*Tess of the d'Urbervilles*, Thomas Hardy

Why is the strawberry so darn delicious?
And who decided to preserve it,
closed up in glass, sealed with a lid?
Sometimes I think I know
how the strawberry feels,
stuck here in this jar of a room,
ceiling overhead, airtight and locking me
in one of those stubborn containers
that has to be whacked
on the counter twenty times, held
under hot water, or pried
with a can opener.
Maybe I just want to keep
all my sweetness inside.
What would you do—
take a knife and spread me
on an English muffin? gobble me down?
make a shortcake out of me? Would you
turn me into a tart? Perhaps
you'd prefer to pluck me,
fresh from the cool, moist garden,
your fingers rummaging for the fruit

of me strewn among the leaves.
Would you watch me ripen
from greenish-white to luscious red?
You could douse me in cream
and serve me with macaroons,
perfectly round little mounds,
almond-scented, and chewy.
Would you pop my heart-shaped flesh
into your mouth and savor my seeds
with the buds of your tongue?
Would you feed me
to your new lover, the way Alex fed Tess—
poor Tess, who fell for the untrue berry
the way Eve fell for the snake of her desire,
the way I fell for what enticed like a peach,
but was hard and bitter as a kumquat?

II

Eve's Diner and Road Stop

After my lover leaves me, goes back
to his wife, first thing I do is swear
off men. Then I pack up my lingerie and point
the car west on Route 66 toward Paradise,

Nevada. Days later, I'm driving in the desert,
don't know where I am, just beginning
to panic when I see it rise up like a mirage—

not one of those modern
jobs with beveled glass and imported tiles,
but a real diner, like the one
in Hopper's *Boulevard of Heartache*.

There's a fly-specked calendar on the wall
and an old poster of Marilyn Monroe,
wind blowing up her skirt.

I don't like to eat alone, a woman on the road,
but this is a woman's diner. Tables for ladies,
none for men. Booth after booth occupied
by a single woman, no men anywhere.

I grab a seat at the counter in between
a babe in a red satin dress
and a biker chick in black leather.

I ask, *Where are the men? Where are the creeps*
and jerks, the halt and lame, truckdrivers,
recovering alcoholics, the unemployed?
This is a diner, for God's sake. A waitress laughs

and says, *Honey, you're on your way to Paradise,*
home of the serpent. Now how about a cup
of coffee and a piece of apple pie?

Dressed in a belly dancer's outfit, she takes
my order, long single braid down her back,
one snake tattooed around her wrist
like a bracelet, another climbing her biceps.

The Blues Going and Coming

She had the blues like flowers have the blues,
the deep rare iridescent blues of irises,
delphiniums, cornflowers, bluebells.

She had the blues like jazz has the blues,
like Coltrane had the blues.
She had the blues like Bessie had the blues
when she sang *Memphis Blues* and *St. Louis Blues*.

She had the blues like Bonnie had the blues
when she knew she'd never see her mother again
because she'd gone so far with Clyde
she could never go home, and she was so blue
she couldn't get off the bed or move,
could only tell Clyde, *I got the blues so bad.*

She had the blues like Picasso had the blues,
when all he could think about was blue,
when every color he put to the canvas was blue.

She had the blues like Monday has the blues,
not once in a blue moon, but all the time.
Oh Lord, she had the blues, she had the blues.

My Father's Garden

In the last days of his life, my father
sends for me, asks to see me one more time.
It's been years since I walked out, swearing
I'd never go back, but I want to
give him one last chance to say he's sorry.

In the hospital room, thick with the stink
of flowers, cancer snakes its way up his
spine. I see his hands, thin and blue, crossed
on the sheets of his bed. He is so old
and sick he couldn't hurt anyone now.

Sitting beside my father while he sleeps,
I see those hands years ago covered with
dirt from his garden, where flowers sprung up
like torches. I see him digging shallow
ditches for seeds and bulbs. In summer,

flowers will stretch for acres. It will look
like Paradise. It will feel like Hell.
In summer, my father will take my
brother and me into his garden because
we are bad children. He will make us strip

off our shirts and stand for hours in the sun,
like prisoners, spikes of gladiolus
so thick no one can see us. We will pass

28

out, we will blister, we will be so sick
our mother will nearly go crazy.

I want to ask my father how hands
that grew flowers could belong to the same
man who hurt children. I want to hear him say
he's sorry. Awake now and nearly blind
with pain, he looks at the nurse and asks, *Is this*

my daughter? He takes my hands in his and
strokes them as if they were kittens. He holds
up his hands to the nurse and says, *You know,*
I never hit my children, not once,
not ever, in all those years.

Point Pleasant Beach, 1948

Remember what they tell you to forget.
—Muriel Rukeyser

She remembers Point Pleasant Beach,
the weekend her father took her there.

It must have been summer.
She remembers the heat.

She remembers the boardwalk,
resistance of wood under her feet,
the ringing and whirring of carousel,
ferris wheel, tilt-a-whirl,
and spinning around and around.

She remembers the taste of taffy,
how her father combed
cotton candy out of her hair.

She remembers waking in the motel
and pulling her father's whiskers
so he'd get up and take her to the beach.

It must have been morning.
She remembers the sun.

She does not remember his muted laughter.
She does not remember the heat of his breath,
nor the feel of his whiskers scraping her cheek.

She remembers only the water,
the sting of salt, slap of waves,
rocking and falling, and something
like undertow pulling her in.

After the Stillbirth

She went down to bedrock—
like a miner, hit the hard place
at the center, trapped
under the heft of stone,
unable to breathe.
Today she hears the sounds
of home—a bird screeching,
plane overhead, newspaper
hitting the porch. She notices
small things—the hose
on the patio, curled
like a snake, a robin shaking
its feathers, lilacs in bloom.
Workmen in hard hats
arrive to top the trees.
Oaks and willows
have grown wild this year,
dangerous in a storm,
her neighbor says. Now a day
of ladders unfolding,
chain saws revving, branches
falling. All day men in talk,
tree talk. A day with a hum
behind it, the smell
of leaves and wood-
scented air. She recalls
the fragrance of peaches

ripening in summer.
It seems to her rough,
elemental work, this cutting
of trees, like blasting
a hole through granite,
and finding some light.

The Barren Woman's Gift

Give me something to love, something living
in the house—a cat, she begs.
Her husband says No, cats are sneaky.
They pee in area rugs and stink
up the house.

For her birthday, he gives a facsimile
of a tabby cat, huge and stuffed with down.
Isis she names it, cradles the fluff in her lap, imagines
growth. She prepares a basket,
adds a soft pillow, a rubber mouse.

She dreams purring, then for many nights,
howling like a great baby, bereft. *There, there,*
she whispers, lifting it against her shoulder
and stroking the haunches.

She settles it in bed between her
and her husband. It chews the top
of her gown, licks her face
with its rough tongue. Paws knead
skin, the spine stiffens with pleasure,

such longing
to kill mice with her teeth. She dumps the bodies
on his side of the bed, chases him away
with her fishy breath.

When he comes
near, she arches her back and hisses,
extends her claws, ready to pounce, dainty mouth
stuffed with feathers and wings.

Cat's-Eyes

I am watching the cat
  watching the birds.
    She wears a collar
      with a tiny silver bell
    and enters my yard as if
  it were her yard. She has
learned of my birdbaths
  and purple martin house,
    a small hotel on a stick.
      Birds perched in trees
    stand lookout for the birds
  pecking the ground. When
the cat appears, a great
  fluttering of wings, agitation
    of leaves, and dozens of birds
      lift to the trees. She hides
    behind an azalea and waits.
  I imagine the longing for a robin,
blackbird, the delicacy of sparrow.
  Pretending to get discouraged,
    she skulks away, circles back,
      moves beneath the purple
    martin house, and lies down
  in grass, still as a pile of leaves.
She spies a cardinal light
  on the rim of the birdbath,
    rises, and shifts one foot

after another, slowly, barely
moving at all. Her whole body
stiffens and undulates. I move
with her, feel the sway and surge
in sinew and fiber, slip inside,
and breathe the scent of bird.
Nothing can stop it now—not
the collar, not the bell, not the birds
in the trees. She clamps down
with teeth, paws the bird, stuffs
her mouth with wings, cartilage,
and blood. Scarlet feathers float.
I watch her sharpen her claws
on the bark of a tree, lick dust
off fur, and taste salt on my tongue,
feel a low rumble deep in my throat.

On First Reading *Romeo and Juliet*

While the rest of us read the death scene,
you twirled your gold-red hair, red
like the inside of a pomegranate,
spun it around
your index finger
in spirals.

                    Maggie,
you didn't know that in a certain light
sun motes glinted
off your hair, not quite copper,
not quite bronze, but something
more rare.

When the bell rang right in the middle
of Romeo's final soliloquy,
you closed your book and tossed
your tresses, all fourteen-year-old
nonchalance, then strolled past Jimmy Dimouli,
the dumb kid who'd read the part of Romeo
you'd ignored.

You made your exit like a star, hair
trailing behind—a fiery comet
showering particles of gold
at Jimmy's feet.

Maggie,
you didn't notice him, star-struck,
spiraling like a solar wind toward Earth,
half a soliloquy stuck in his throat.

The Missing Remote

Not lost or mislaid, but hidden.
While you were in Florida chasing
golf balls, I took possession
of your baton. I wanted
the thrill of clutching it,
night after night, pushing buttons
shaped like miniature nipples,
longed to mute the noise
and not listen, the way you don't
listen to me. I wanted the power
in my lap, my hand, needed
to turn on and turn off, and I did,
multiple times. I raised and lowered
the volume, returned to the previous
channel, grew dizzy with pictures
leaping, colors flashing, red, yellow,
and green. I positioned myself
in front of the screen and feasted
on sandwiches and snatches
of commercials, the tail end
of a third quarter, the opening
round of a game show. I tasted
reality. I enjoyed everything in bits
and pieces, as if nibbling
from a box of Godiva chocolates.
It wasn't *NYPD Blue* or *ER* or even
Judge Judy I craved, but the force

of that glossy little rectangle.
And now you're back, missing
your gizmo. You'll never touch
those delicate buttons again.
You'll stretch out in your favorite
recliner, night after night, unfrocked,
while I'm a swirl of primary colors
and spinning all over the globe.

The Intimacy of Laundry

After the Ecstasy, the Laundry
—Jack Kornfield

Buzzed awake in a comfortable
        chair, I watch my husband folding
    underwear. He separates his boxers

from my underpants as if they're not allowed
        to play with each other,
    stacks the boxers in quarters, and attacks

my panties. It's one of those dry days,
        fall air full of static electricity.
    Everything he touches

crackles and jolts. My panties are loose
        and wild, flying and flinging themselves
    at him, clinging, one on each arm,

one on his chest, another grabbing
        his crotch. He peels them off,
    turns them right side out, cotton lining

demurely tucked inside. He shakes
        and smooths
    their wrinkles, builds a slippery mound

beside the tower of boxers, holds
            the last pair against his face as if
       listening to a secret, and pulls my panties

down, slowly, across his whiskery skin.
            Every cell in my body
       registers the voltage. I curse

my plain white nylon briefs,
            wish for black lace
       or some unholy shade of red.

Losing the Blues

Stuck in traffic and lost
without you, I see it on a bumper sticker:
Wild women don't get the blues. Swerving

off the highway, I pull up to a neon
martini glass, order a shot of tequila. I suck
salt with a lemon wedge, slip

on a red satin dress, nail taps to my spikes, fasten
       castanets to my thumbs. I eat rare meat
           and all seven layers of a devil's food cake.

I hardly remember your name.

                  Chartreuse
      flows through my veins. I'm every color on the palette
but blue. I'm so hot I'm cool. I spit
       in the street, and men swoon

when I do it. No more jazz for me, no rhythm
       and blues, no gospel, no country, no soul. I'm all
rock 'n' roll. I hang out

with gangsters, play the ponies, and encourage
       my urges. I'm no shade of blue—
          no sky, no periwinkle, sapphire, or indigo.

I'll never again be royal for you.

I'm cerise, vermilion, scarlet,
ruby, crimson, fuchsia, magenta,
and flame. I could burn
the hands off a man.

Eve's Red Dress

I hang
deep in her closet,
red
as any apple she's ever bitten.

She wants to slip
into me. Her mother's voice says, *No.*
Red is not your color, not good
with your hair, your face, your eyes.
Her mother would dress her in blue,
but she's been blue so long. I shimmer
and sparkle, the perfect size
and luscious.

She reaches for me,
imagines how I would slide onto her
like skin. She knows she would be
sensational in me. She longs for my satin,
my deep neckline, my thin straps, rope of black
pearls around her neck.

She wants
to go dancing in me—tango, bossa nova,
merengue—my skirt fanning out like brushfire,
her mother's words smouldering in ashes, wants
to burst like a fireball onto the floor, spinning
and whirling, my skirt singing, *Touch me and burn.*

The Mystery of the Missing Girl

The summer my mother sent me away,
I became a girl detective and searched
my grandmother's attic. Like Nancy Drew,
I carried a flashlight and crept
over creaky boards, investigated
rooms and passages. It was a dark space,
no windows, no air, full of cobwebs and secrets,
a place for a ghost.

While Hannah baked bread in the kitchen, I pried
open a door and found what I'd come for—evidence
of my mother's childhood.
I sat on her bed, held tight to the rails
of the headboard, and tracked
her trail—

Tinted photograph of my mother
standing in a row of girls, all claiming
innocence. Pencil box with hinged lid,
like a miniature coffin, pencils missing
erasers, teeth marks in the wood.
Green jumper, pocket sewn with the insignia
of the Lakewood Academy for Girls.
One copy of *Jane Eyre*, chapel scene
dog-eared, as if she'd planned to return,
and in the margin, *Such grief!* decipherable.

I slipped into the jumper and went undercover,
then beamed my light across the room.
A wedding dress, preserved in a plastic bag,
hung from a hook, like a sack of bones.

I unzipped the bag and touched the dress.
A girl stepped out in white satin, her face familiar
and wanted. I looked close for the upcurved
red lips, the iridescent eyes of her smile.

My Grandmother's Bed Jacket

On Sundays my grandmother stayed in bed.
She wasn't like other children's grandmothers.
She didn't tell stories, and though she was old,
her skin wasn't wrinkled. She painted her nails
and wore rings with stones that had names
like tourmaline, aquamarine, and amethyst.
She'd lost a son in the war, and her hair was blue.

On Sundays my grandmother wore a bed jacket,
a delicate half-bathrobe made of silk and lace.
She sat propped against the mahogany
headboard, pillows fluffed, ladies' magazines
spread out like Tarot cards—*Harper's Bazaar*,
Vanity Fair, *Better Homes and Gardens*—
and on her bureau a photograph of a boy.

What I wanted to see was the huge oxygen tank
next to her bed. It stood like a misplaced torpedo.
A black hose hung out, attached to a plastic mask.
I could hear wheezing and rattling in her chest.
Sometimes she lifted the mask to her face,
leaned back the blue glow of her hair, and gasped
for air. Then she breathed, in, out, in, out.

My father called his mother the old battle-ax,
said she was spoiled and cold. When she died
at sixty-two, my grandfather remembered her

as a bride, the most beautiful girl he'd ever seen.
What I remember is the way her fingers sparkled
as she held the photograph, and the elegance
of her bed jacket, how it rose and fell when she breathed.

The Changing Room

The old man stood next to my blanket,
blocking the sun. His wife clung to his arm.
They must have been ninety,
fragile as sticks.

New mother that summer, I thought they'd come
to admire my baby. Instead, the old man held out
a swimsuit, asked me to change
his wife. Strip down some ancient stranger?
I had never seen my own mother
naked—but the suit was already in my hand,
the woman grabbing my arm.

In the changing room, she leaned
on me. I pulled off her slacks, unbuttoned
the blouse. She wore no bra. Two thin flaps
of flesh, husks of breasts, stretched below her waist,
each with a tiny nipple like a bead.

I thought of my own full breasts,
nipples swollen like corks and leaking milk,
my infant's joyful sucking.

I left on her underpants, like a diaper,
and pulled up the suit, inch by inch,
not wanting to rip her paper-thin flesh,
not minding its mushroom scent.

With slower steps, I escorted her back.
Her husband patted her hand and said,
Oh sweetheart, my sweetheart. They waded
into water up to their necks, his face
suffused with sunlight, hers
luminous, and where the sticks of their fingers
touched, I could almost swear I saw sparks.

As they bobbed up and down, barely floating
in this world, I watched over her,
protective and anxious as any new mother,
ready, if she needed me, to leap
into water and pull her back.

First Cold

Rales of phlegm rattled the midnight air.
The baby all stuffed up, asleep in his crib.
Later his crying, different this time—
a sad crying, not meaning, *Feed me.*
I'd never felt flesh so hot. He burned
like a cinder. I watched the thermometer rise
to 104°, and I froze, then ran to the phone
to call my husband, still in transition
between single and married.

I dialed the bar where I knew he'd be.
A stranger answered. I could hear music
and laughter. The voice on the phone was drunk.
I said my husband's name, *Is he there?*
The voice wanted to make jokes—
Who wants to know? What's it worth to you?
I asked again, *Please, is he there?* and began
to cry, *Please, my baby is sick,* and the man
became sober, said, *Hold on, lady, just hold on,*
and he found my husband and sent him home.

For hours we took turns dipping the baby
into tepid water, as if bronzing him.
Toward dawn the fever broke, and our baby
peed. An arc of urine rose like a fountain
and fell, tinged the water yellow.

My husband and I faced each other
across the plastic tub, gazed in mute wonder
at the small priest who'd come to bless
and curse us both, two strangers,
hardly knowing our names.

Jesus Performs Yet Another Miracle

Our bodies weren't made to take showers
in wine, she said.
What did she mean by that?
Had she turned on the faucet one morning
and wine poured forth?
Had Jesus come back as a plumber?

Or perhaps she'd walked in rain one afternoon
wearing her new white jacket.
Perhaps she'd noticed rivulets of scarlet
rolling off her shoulders like stigmata.
Had she looked up and seen beaujolais
coming out of thunder clouds?

Imagine the potential in this new millennium.
We might order a storm with a prayer:
God, spritz me with a light zinfandel,
or *God, please rain on my parade—*
hearty burgundy would be fine—
or *Dear God, a shower of chardonnay*
once we get settled on the beach.

None of us would ever again forget
to brush our teeth, now an act of oblation.
We'd worship at the sink, our morning toast
a wafer, the water cup a chalice,

the simple act of cleansing the body
a form of prayer.

Daily we would commune with the Lord
in gratitude and grace, amazed each time
by the miracle of transfiguration.

But think again: no rained out games, no ruined
vacations or graduations, so much less to gripe
about. We'd all be walking around
with our tongues hanging out, heads
tilted back, eyes
raised to the sky, and crying,
Oh, Sweet Jesus, pelt me with rain.

Superman Flies

You think it's easy—
all that flying? Leaping
over tall buildings,
never landing
on a steeple?
Try stopping a train
with your hand. Try
being super at anything.
People expect so much
from greatness. You're always
being asked to perform
miracles, like you're Jesus
or something. And suppose
you love a woman,
and when she looks
at you, you melt, as if
she'd held up a piece
of kryptonite.
Ever tried stripping
in a telephone booth
in three seconds flat?
Now that's a miracle.
So's her face, her eyes,
her friendly thighs.
Some days x-ray vision
is a blessing, some days
a curse. Imagine

trying to look
manly in a cape. Imagine her
wrapped in your cape, bare
arms stretched out
straight ahead, her hand
holding a piece
of your heart, the two of you flying
over some flaming metropolis.
With the fate of a nation
in your hands, you hold on
to what you have yearned for
and let the city burn.

Waiting for the Streetcar

A man stands on the street below me,
waiting for the streetcar that doesn't stop
here anymore. He's swarthy, muscular,
grimy with sweat, an animal in a red satin
bowling shirt. He grasps a beer bottle
in his fist, rips off the cap with his teeth,
and spits in the street.

He's the kind who hurls radios from windows,
smashes lightbulbs, drinks too much and loses
control, roughs up his woman, takes her
like a brute, a primal man bringing home
the raw meat.

He's standing on the street below me,
calling and calling my name.

Crazy Larry

I want to be crazy like Larry is crazy,
Larry who does not keep quiet about his desperation
but flails in the street, accosts
strangers, and does not say, *Help me,*
but foams and drools and staggers,
drunk on his madness, in collusion with demons,
and who, no matter how many times we lock him up,
keeps coming back,
who will not take his medicine or help himself,
will not change his attitude or think positive thoughts,
but kicks, screams, and bites,
and will not lie down on the therapist's couch
and will not be restrained
even when he's four-pointed on the hospital bed,
stretched out like a compass or that man on a medieval map,
a spread-eagled Jesus,
who cannot throw off the beast on his chest
and is terrified every minute of every day,
but opens his mouth and roars,
who is not half-assed crazy, but crazy all the way,
crazy with conviction, crazy like he means it.

She Provides Her Therapist with a History

Slut's wool under the bed.
Piles of it—this, she says, is why her lover left.
She's heard of women who make dolls to ward off
evil. Says she could use a doll like that.
She dreams of Barbie
with a machine gun.
Practices Zen, spends hours chanting, "The top of my head
supports heaven." Says some days the weight
is insupportable. Some days believes
Chicken Little was right: the sky *is* falling.
She remembers feeling sad watching her lover eat wings.
All week she has longed
for cherry tomatoes.
In the park she sees dragonflies make love
on the wing. She compliments them
on the economy
of their desire. She is reminded of her lover
who is an airline pilot.
She remembers the day he left, remembers staring
at the laces on her sneakers, thinking
how frayed they were.
She remembers a man
who bumped into her at the 7-Eleven. He'd said,
"You'll have to forgive me. I've been in a car accident,
and I'm still putting myself back together," then crashed
his way through the store. She longs
for the capacity to forgive.

Her favorite author is James Thurber whose work
she has not read
but who as a child hearing that the girl next door
had cried her heart out went to look for it.
She imagines posters
hammered onto telephone poles: *Have you seen this heart?*

The Bat

I was a woman alone in a country
     of bears and not particularly brave.
          Adrift on the periphery of a dream,

          I heard a vague flapping noise,
     swoosh, swoosh, against the screen.
A huge expanse of wing—butterfly

in giant proportion—glided across
     the room, back and forth, back
          and forth, weightless on air.

          I might have admired the precision
     and grace, but I was afraid for my hair,
afraid of the terrible teeth, rabies, and

madness. I flipped on the light, became
     a small god, a woman who can shift
          day and night. My hand holding fire,

          I sit up all night, fully awake, night after
     night, a woman alone on the edge
of a dream. Its brief flight ended,

it hangs over my head, upside
     down on the ceiling still, fingers
          and toes gripped to the rafter, soaring

wings folded along the mouse-like
body, puffing away in perpetual sleep,
echoing at a frequency only I

can hear, its punishment to endlessly
wonder whatever happened to the
night, the dark and mastered air.

IV

Eve's Confession

Sunday morning I slipped
out of bed, ran to the bakery,
and bought two apple
fritters—huge, bulging
with fruit, and slathered
with sweet white frosting—
breakfast in bed for me
and my husband.
          While he slept on
in innocence, his ribcage
peacefully rising
and falling, the kitchen
filled with essence
of apple. And oh!
those fritters looked
divine. I broke
off a sample—wickedly
good—then another
and another.
          Of course, it was
my husband's fritter
I sampled. I stuffed
my mouth. Globs
of tart gooey apples slid
down my throat, apple
after apple, and chunks

of dough, crusty
from the fryer.
       I could feel
my cholesterol rising,
arteries hardening, and I
didn't care. That fritter
was delicious.
       As the calories
mounted, guilt entered
the kitchen. And still,
that pastry beguiled me.
"Eat of this fritter," it called.
"Okay," I said, "one last bite,"
but knew I was going to fall
and fall, knew in my evil
heart I was going
to eat it all.

The Study of Nature

Every morning for thirty years you've kissed me,
the same kiss, one neat peck, chaste

as toast. Look through the window.
Take a lesson from the cat that visits our yard:

Hide in the bushes. Be still, every muscle poised.
Observe me as I stroll across the patio and enter

the garden, your ears raised and stiff, as if listening
to some ancient primal call, some deep-throated

growl. Catch the scent of my heated blood drifting
through leaves. Let it tickle the touch organs

of your whiskers. Size me up. Picture your mouth
stuffed. Think of the different ways

to take me. When I've bent over to smell a rose
or nibble a berry, unaware of your upraised fur,

the vertical lift of your tail, sneak out of the bushes,
one paw in front of the other. Go slow, glide,

as if not moving at all. Imagine me all catnip
and cream. Then pounce. Lick me

with your rough tongue. Make me pray
for mercy. Devour me down to the bone.

Feeding Habits

At Ecco-la, my husband orders a bottle
　　of Louis Jadot chardonnay. While he studies
the menu, I glance across the room.
　　A young couple waits at the bar, drinking
beer. The guy leans over and kisses his girl,
　　a short sweet kiss, like an hors d'oeuvre,
then a long kiss, their arms wrapped
　　around each other, his fingers caught
in the strands of her hair. My husband and I
　　debate appetizers and entrees. They feast
on each other. By the time the waiter returns
　　to take our orders, I'm practically starving.
Soon he sets before me a plate
　　of scallops, shrimp, and arugula, tossed
in scampi sauce, and nestled on a bed
　　of linguini. They're kissing again. She nestles
her head against his chest. He strokes
　　the skin of her arm. I pop a scallop
into my mouth, savor the succulent flesh, then fork
　　a shrimp, pass it to my husband. He offers a bite
of portobello mushroom stuffed
　　with king crab, seasoned with herbs and a hint
of lemon. We consume and consume.
　　Across the room an ear is nibbled,
cheeks and neck devoured. I beg my husband
　　for dessert. He holds up his hand to say
he's had enough for one night. I seduce him
　　into chocolate mousse pie with a layer

of meringue, order charlotte russe for myself.
　With the recklessness of Sybarites,
we fill our mouths with ladyfingers, whipped cream,
　and chocolate curls. Nothing, nothing ever tasted
this good. As the couple is led to their table,
　my husband and I head for home, still licking
our lips, our tongues searching for crumbs.

A Year Without Rock 'n' Roll

Was it something in the air, some toxin we breathed in,
or out? Mrs. Colvin's baby died that year,
the Jacksons' dog bit Danny Edelman
and was put to sleep, my father
disappeared.

We were like one of those neighborhoods
where all the kids get leukemia or the women
breast cancer and men in orange rescue suits
dig up the ground, looking for the spot
where sorrow begins.

My mother sat by the phonograph and filled our house
with jazz and blues. I wanted *Dancing
in the Streets* and *Piece of My Heart*. I wanted
Rescue Me, but we were all
Mood Indigo.

Last night I heard the screech of a cat
in heat. It went on for hours, such longing
of the body for some other cat.
The pillow next to me empty now for a year,
I felt that longing, a song
my body sings—

*Come on and rescue me,
'cause I'm lonely and I'm blue—*

and this morning the drone of a garbage truck,
the staccato beep beep beep as it backed
down the hill, get up, get up, get up,
day coming awake, the otherworldly hum
of migratory geese, tremulous vibrato
of wings in flight.

Reading the Signs

I want to read the love letters my mother burned,
the ones my father wrote before they married.

Could the man I remember have said
something romantic?—found a garden
in her face, lilies and cherries, or like Romeo,
compared her eyes to stars?
Would he have pined under a heartless moon,
said he needed her as roses need sun?

He once gave my mother
a geode—hard granite exterior, cavity inside
spilling out amethysts—
profusion of lavender and purple.

My father hurled words like rocks,
would have said something like,
Susan, I want you
here, now. Come back, and this time, stay,
and she, foolish woman, would have felt
a tremor, and thought him a man
who could move heaven and earth.

Service for the Murdered Boy

In Tibet they lay their dead
on the side of a mountain.

All night I dream of the murdered boy
decomposing in the Himalayas,
laid out under a Banyan tree.
No monsoon of grief in this unarable land,
only mountains rumbling
with footsteps of tigers, snow leopards,
and moon bears. A hundred vultures fill the sky.
All circle in, nuzzle the boy with snouts and beaks,
and devour him until nothing's left but bones
and a skull, resting on stones hard as fists.

I dream a mission of monks, roaming
the desert, spinning prayer wheels,
and searching peasant villages for the right
boy, the one birthed at the exact moment
of death. They lift the born-again buddha
and carry him home.

But my dream lasts only as long as the night.
Morning brings echoes of *Ave Maria.*

The father's wearing a red jacket
with white leather sleeves, the kind
boys wear when they make the varsity team.

He leans into the mike and says,
"I don't want to talk about the future,
or games that won't get played,
or the boy who shot him. I want to talk
about songs that were sung."
Then he breaks down, turns to his son
still smiling in the blown-up photograph.

I don't want church music, soft and mournful.
I want hard rock, heavy metal,
music all bass and treble, cranked up full blast,
the kind that blares out windows of cars
driven by boys, the kind that rocks
the ground and trembles the earth with their songs.

When News Comes of a Child's Death

You think you couldn't bear it,
your child dying,
think you couldn't survive.

But God will not grant you that small mercy.
You will rise and function.
You will make the necessary arrangements—
pick the plot of ground,
select the wood, and order the stone.
You will accept food from the mourners.
And yes, you will consume.

You will pay the bills,
write the notes, push the vacuum,
and clean out the room.

For two years you will not look at other people's children.

Then in spring you will walk.
You will see grass growing,
and you will be amazed—

doesn't the grass know?
doesn't the mute, dumb grass know?—

and always you will stand braced,
as in that still moment between
the thunder clap and the lightning bolt.

Miscarriage

I had not come to kill them,
only to see the blue eggs in the nest.
I waited until the mother flew out,
then went with a stick to nudge them a bit—
three tiny eggs, the color of sky, speckled with white.

Something in me that summer could not bear
perfection. Something had happened
to my mother. She'd been gone a long time.
My father's whispered words hovered like dragonflies—
miscarriage, fallopian tubes, hysterectomy.

I touched my stick to one of the shells
and pushed. I heard the pip-pip of the rupture—
another, and another. I saw the life
in the shells—three tiny fetuses, each covered with slime,
and inside, still pulsing, a black eye like a bead.

Mrs. VanNess came out of her house shouting,
Don't touch! She saw what I'd done
and chased me away. I was a wicked girl, she yelled.
She would tell my parents. I'd be tormented
by nightmares. I would roast in hell.

My mother rested in the shade under a tree.
My father brought her iced tea and lemon cookies
with poppy seeds. She looked like the antique doll

held behind glass at the museum, limbs rigid,
her face crazed china.

I wanted to tell her what I'd done, to climb into her lap
and confess. My father wouldn't let me
touch her. He must have known she'd break.
I wanted to tell her I'd seen the babies
with their terrible, terrible eyes.

Cracked

Was it really about a broken egg?
And why was Humpty Dumpty sitting on that wall?
White ovoid, ridiculous in suit and tie.
Not a hard-boiled detective like the guy in *The Maltese Falcon*,
just an egg, no curled fetus of bird in the shell,
only firm flesh gripping the nugget inside.
Something must have been flying overhead—
shadow of wings, a sulphurous cloud, the caw-caw of crows,
darkness below, and we are so small,
my brother and I—Easter,
no rabbit, no basket, no resurrection this year.
Our father is gone, no coming back this time,
and my brother has dropped the egg splat on the floor,
and our gentle mother hits him, and says, *Christ, oh Christ,*
and begins to cry,
soft, like the peep-peep of a bird that has fallen and cracked
its wing and can't ever be put back together again.

Imelda's Shoes

My closet, too, bulges
with shoes—espadrilles,
pumps, platforms, slingbacks,
and spikes, shoes that bring corns,
blisters, bunions, and bone spurs, faithless
shoes that couldn't hold up in a storm, deceitful
shoes, in the store as soft as butter, torture chambers
evermore, shoes that squeeze the balls of my feet, shoes
with leather uppers, manmade soles, backless, strapless,
toeless, shoes with buttons, belts, and hooks, shoes
with tongues that do not speak, white satin slippers
still in a box, tissue folded like wings, so many
shoes to fill, each a reproach, lined up like
husks of locust. Yes, I have known desire
for shoes, the need to enclose space,
tie up and lace, tuck in the tongue,
and quietly slip away.

The Missing Wife

Wife and dog missing.
Reward for the dog.
　　　—bumper sticker on a pickup truck

The wife and the dog planned their escape
months in advance, laid up biscuits and bones,
waited for the careless moment when he'd forget
to latch the gate, then hightailed it.

They took shelter in the forest, camouflaged
the scent of their trail with leaves.
Free of him at last,
they peed with relief on a tree.

Time passed. They came and went as they pleased,
chased sticks when they felt like chasing sticks,
dug holes in what they came to regard
as their own backyard. They unlearned
how to roll over and play dead.

In spring the dog wandered off in pursuit
of a rabbit. Collared by a hunter and returned
to the master for $25, he lives
on a tight leash now. He sleeps
on the wife's side of the bed,
whimpering, pressing his snout

into her pillow, breathing the scent
of her hair.

And the wife? She's moved deep into the heart
of the forest. She walks
on all fours, fetches for no man, performs
no tricks. She is content. Only sometimes
she gets lonely, remembers how he would nuzzle
her cheek and comfort her when she twitched
and thrashed in her sleep.

V

Eve's Own Garden

There are children who eat dirt, a disease
the doctors who tend them call Pica. The doctors
suspect such children crave the iron found in soil.

This is my secret: I have feasted
on dirt. A garden grows inside me, not
all earthly delights—gladiolus, big sloppy
blossoms, yellow, pink, magenta—
funeral flowers, the flowers my father grew,
the ones my mother made me promise
not to put on her grave.
                            And roses, I bloom
roses, not American Beauties, but sweetbriers
so wild and profuse they bleed
over the fence, blood-red, scarlet, crimson.
My roses have Japanese beetles.
No matter the poison I spray, they keep
coming back. I have grown
to love my beetles.
                            I sprout spikes
of delphiniums, irises, and larkspur, blue
so blue it's almost purple. I cultivate
blue, let it wrap itself inside me
like vines.
                Of course
there's a snake. What's a garden

without a snake, a spring
                    and a fall?
He insinuates himself among the stones, slithers
through tendrils of veins, vessels, and fiber.
This is fertile ground, and wholly
mine. I have plowed and hoed
and dug shallow ditches.
                    Snapdragons,
sweetpeas, fireweed, bird
of paradise rise by onion grass, skunk cabbage,
mushrooms, and moss, all nurtured by loam
and well-rotted manure. This is no bower
of bliss.
            Yes, I have bitten
dirt, savored the sweet metallic taste of soil.
I want what the earth has. Yes, I eat dirt.
It tastes good on my floral tongue.

The Barren Woman's Dream

And Rachel said unto Jacob, Give me
children, or else I die.
                    —Genesis 30:1

When the doctor said, *No, not ever,*
she nodded as if she understood,
took to her bed, and would not get up.

Late that night she and her husband
lay together in the fallow field
and scattered their seed on the fertile ground.

All winter long she bided her time,
knitting bonnets and booties,
like other women did, but by the hundreds.

In spring the first heads emerged,
shooting up like carrots
with tufts of fuzz on the crowns.

All summer she labored in the field,
shooing away rabbits and crows,
watching her crop multiply.

By summer's end, a field of babies
swayed like wheat in the Iowa breeze,
a bountiful harvest of babies.

They reached their arms out to her,
all perfect, all beautiful,
her hunger ripening inside her.

Eating My Words

I have plucked them from my garden
and my neighbor's too, a basketful
of syllables. Some I eat fresh from the soil,
like a rabbit raiding a lettuce patch. Delicious
dirty words—lascivious, licentious, libidinous.

Some go on windowsills to ripen
in sun. Others I put up in Mason jars
and store like nuts in a squirrel's nest,
sustenance for the winter ahead.

I am assisted by my lover, a former librarian.
We shape inkhorn terms from raw
syllables, blend compounds with hyphens,
roll out malapropisms. We pour chilled sidereal
into long-stemmed crystal, wrap our tongues
around salacious and salubrious.

My star-flanked lover offers a slice
of pizzicato. I pass the glissando.
We eat predaciously, two athletes
of the soul, feeding our desire
to speak. Words tumble out in a stew
of confusion—bluegrass, hoodoo, bushwhack,
incubus and succubus, bedrock, serendipity,
silly putty, tatterdemalion, violet, and lavender.

We savor each frangible, incendiary syllable,
swishing and squishing them in our mouths,
picking out plangent caught between our teeth.

Dessert, a lubricious savannah,
we garnish with ictus and nimbus.
My lover is all slipstream, I am all spindrift.
Together we are perfectly flummoxed.
No rebarbatives after this feast, only a filament
and a tumbler of smooth sprezzatura.

Fruitless

The sign at the market says,
"No plums today."
Right away I feel plums,
ripe and chilled, in the palm of my hand.
No other fruit will do—
not cherries, not berries, not even peaches.

Mr. Lopez picks up a peach,
fingers its fuzz, squeezes, and says,
"Where you friend? Why he no come with you?"
I tell him you're somewhere else today.
He presses the fruit into my hand,
but I want plums

or nothing at all. It's just that way with plums.
Not satisfied with a peach,
I leave empty-handed,
waving goodby, goodby. Mr. Lopez says,
"You friend, maybe come back other day."
Fruitless and longing for something to do,

I walk in the park, no longer with you,
palm to palm,
Romeo and Juliet's holy palmers' kiss. That yesterday
I want back again. I want the touch,
the plum of your tongue and what it said.
I remember your hands

stroking my hair, how every strand
felt important. I once showed you
a pair of cardinals, birds mated for life. You said
my red hair was like plumage.
I wanted scarlet birds to teach us
fidelity, like a plumb line, vertical and true. Today

the three of us are missing you. Today
the sky overhead
is raucous with the screeches
of starlings. It's never been this blue.
I am hungry for plums,
the skin of them, the tang, and the scent.

You always preached *Carpe diem.*
Look hard now at the trees and see as I do—
the ghosts of plums hang in the branches.

On the Use of Concrete Language

Don't say love. Say switchblade.
—Peter Murphy

She remembers the click
and the snap of it
when he opened the blade,
and the black of his
eyes when he flipped it
through his fingers like
some kind of juggler,
and the heat of it,
yes, the heat of it.

She remembers the twinge
sharp as the blade held
to her throat, dragged down
her arm, teasing, circling
the breasts, down her belly,
how it grazed the soft fur
of her skin, and the chill
of the steel, how she shivered.

He put it right to the heart.
He was going to leave
marks, and later, scars.

The first shudder
of flesh and the blade
of his body, the slip
and the slide of it,
he carved inside her,
the words he stuck
in her throat.

The Properties of Light

Isn't the whole world heaven's coast?
— from *Heaven's Coast*, Mark Doty

I come for the light, the artist says.
Dawn and again at sunset,
he goes to the Provincetown beach,
sets up his easel. At just the right angle,
he can catch that light on the canvas.

He uses words like *shimmer, glow, radiance.*
He talks about what our forefathers must have seen
when they woke that first dawn just off the coast.
He darkens the room, lights up the wall
with his slides. We see
not the play of light against dark,
but the play of light against light.
We see it in the rocks, the beached whale,
the bones of dead fish.

In the last days of my father's life,
he kept calling me—*Elaine, Elaine*—
even though I was in the next room
or the same room and he didn't need
or want anything. He kept doing it.
If I answered, he'd know
he was still alive. If I didn't,
he was dead.

The last time he called, he held out
his hand, all blue veins and bones now.
His head fell back, and the skin
on his face smoothed out.

What I remember is the light,
how it slipped into the room and took him.
In that moment, the light was different,
and I saw my father as I had never seen
him before—young, full of wonder,
and in no pain at all.

Pastiche for a Daughter's Absence

It all comes down to what's physical,
this missing her—her face, voice, and skin.
I imagine my daughter dancing in Madrid, Barcelona,
and Seville, climbing the mountains of Andalusia.
I had not imagined how far away faraway would be.

Happiness, unhappiness—the same,
my sweet Zen master says,
and I wonder if the top of my head
supports heaven, or is this a migraine
coming on?

I circle back to the place where precision
and ecstasy meet, remember how I carried the tadpole
of her body, long before the first flutter, holding her
like a secret inside me.

I wake in the night missing
a body part, my arm stretched across the ocean,
hooked to the past, and I wonder,
as Achilles' mother must have,
Which part of you did I not dip in the water?

Heavy with absence, I hang curtains in her windows,
yards and yards of delicate Irish lace.
I hide behind the door, ear pressed to the wood,

and watch my daughter's life—her evening *paseo,*
late dinners in Saragossa's village square.
The room fills with the smell of *gazpacho, paella, sangria.*

Something like grief washes through me, something like joy.
I slip into the waves, feel the ebb and flow of her,
my water sprite, my sea nymph, remember the way
she glides through a room, the low-tide
of her voice, how she leaves us,
breathless, all fish at her feet.

Her Daughter's Feet

My friend Sally was obsessed
with her baby's feet—the soft dough
of the soles, the ten pea-sized toes—
and because she knew they'd change,
she painted portraits of the feet, canvas
after canvas. Sometimes she dipped the soles
in paint and pressed them onto paper,
like a nurse making hospital footprints.

Feet walked the walls of the house—
feet in water,
           in leaves,
                        feet floating in air.
Chartreuse, turquoise, burnt sienna—
everything shone—nails
painted in silver and gold, feet bejeweled
with anklets and rings, toes with streamers
of ribbons.
                And some of the feet had wings.

The year her daughter disappeared,
Sally stared at the walls, at her daughter's feet,
stared like a tracker looking for a trail.
I thought then of the daughters of China,
their feet bound in yards of cloth, trained to walk
on the wrong bones, unable to dance
or run.

I looked again at those walls,
grown cold as stone, wished hard
for a scattering of seeds, noticed
once more the delicate brushstrokes,
the precision of wings.

The Mathematics of Your Leaving

Today I remembered my algebra book
flying across the room,
my father shouting I was stupid,
a dumb girl, because I couldn't
do math—

and all because you are leaving,
I'm calculating numbers,
totaling years, even
working out equations:
If $x + 1 = 2$, what is the value
of x alone?

All day I've been thinking about
word problems: If a train travels west
at the speed of 60 miles per hour
against a 30 mile per hour wind, how fast
will you be gone?

Today I've added and subtracted,
multiplied and divided. I've mastered
fractions. Even that theorem
I could never understand—plus 1
plus minus 1 equals zero—
is perfectly clear.

Then just when I think I've finally
caught on, a whiz kid now, a regular
Einstein, suddenly the numbers
betray me. No matter how many times
I count the beads on the abacus, work it out
on the calculator, everything comes
to nothing.

Mute and fractured, a dumb girl again,
I sit alone at my desk, staring
out the window, homework
incomplete. A square root unrooted,
I contemplate infinity.

Last Dance

The summer my father waltzed
out of our lives,
I found an old hat buried
in my mother's closet—
black satin, stiff with age,
stitched with tiny silver sequins.

My mother, still in flannel robe,
hair uncombed, said it was the Charleston hat
she'd worn as a girl when she danced
to the big jazz bands—years before
she met my father. *Show me,* I said.

She put it on and began to dance,
steps tentative—a convalescent
learning to walk again. Her arms
flapped like bird wings. Her hands
made circles in the air. She knocked
her knees together, in, out, in, out.

Faster and faster, feet beat time
to music I couldn't hear. Sequins
sparkled in her hair. She twirled, spun,
and seemed to fly, for that moment
airlifted out of her life.

She threw off her robe and shimmied.
Rows of fringe swayed across her red satin
chemise. Feet kicked air. Sparks shot out
from under her shoes. My mother
danced on fire. The crowd moved back
to give more room. The band played
just for her. All eyes were on my mother,
and all around her fire, fire, fire.

My Husband Discovers Poetry

Because my husband would not read my poems,
I wrote one about how I did not love him.
In lines of strict iambic pentameter,
I detailed his coldness, his lack of humor.
It felt good to do this.

Stanza by stanza, I grew bolder and bolder.
Towards the end, struck by inspiration,
I wrote about my old boyfriend,
a boy I had not loved enough to marry
but who could make me laugh and laugh.
I wrote about a night years after we parted
when my husband's coldness drove me from the house
and back to my old boyfriend.
I even included the name of a seedy motel
well-known for hosting quickies.
I have a talent for verisimilitude.

In sensuous images, I described
how my boyfriend and I stripped off our clothes,
got into bed, and kissed and kissed,
then spent half the night telling jokes,
many of them about my husband.
I left the ending deliberately ambiguous,
then hid the poem away
in an old trunk in the basement.

You know how this story ends,
how my husband one day loses something,
goes into the basement,
and rummages through the old trunk,
how he uncovers the hidden poem
and sits down to read it.

But do you hear the strange sounds
that floated up the stairs that day,
the sounds of an animal, its paw caught
in one of those traps with teeth of steel?
Do you see the wounded creature
at the bottom of the stairs,
his shoulders hunched over and shaking,
fist in his mouth and choking back sobs?
It was my husband paying tribute to my art.

About the Author

Diane Lockward is the author of a chapbook, *Against Perfection*, published by Poets Forum Press in 1998. Her poems have appeared in a number of journals, including *Spoon River Poetry Review, The Literary Review, Poet Lore, Cumberland Poetry Review,* and *The Beloit Poetry Journal.* Her work has been nominated twice for a Pushcart Prize and has received awards from *North American Review, Louisiana Literature,* the Newburyport Art Association, and the Akron Art Museum. Her poems have been featured on *Poetry Daily* and read by Garrison Keillor on NPR's *The Writer's Almanac.* In 2001, Lockward was one of ten featured poets at the Warren County Poetry Festival in Blairstown, New Jersey.

A former high school English teacher, Lockward served as an educational consultant to the PBS video series, *Poetry Heaven,* and has been the recipient of three artist-educator scholarships to the Fine Arts Work Center in Provincetown, Massachusetts. She currently works as a poet-in-the-schools for both the New Jersey State Council on the Arts and the Geraldine R. Dodge Foundation.

The mother of three grown children, Lockward lives in West Caldwell, New Jersey, with her husband, Lew.

Printed in the United States
993900002B